Dr. Cecilia Jackson

STEP BACK TO SPRINT FORWARD

God's Biblical Prototypes for Moving Forward Today

Dr. Cecilia Jackson

STEP BACK TO SPRINT FORWARD
God's Biblical Prototypes for Moving Forward Today

© Copyright: First Edition 2011, 2013, 2014
Library of Congress by: Dr. Cecilia Jackson
Printed in the United States of America

All Rights Reserved. No part of this publication may be translated, reproduced, or transmitted in any form or by any means electronic or mechanical, including photocopying, recording, or any information storage and retrieval system, without permission in writing from the author. For information e-mail Dr. Cecilia Jackson at preachers_dd3@yahoo.com.

Scripture quotations from the King James Translation Bible; no source notations required.

Dr. Cecilia Jackson

Introduction

Basic starting techniques are vitally important in sprint races. When one is a successful runner, his success is because of his basic foot position on the starting blocks. The heel will be off the back block, with lots of pressure going through the back foot as a foundational position. Often runners STEP BACK and LOOK BACK in order to secure that they are in proper position to finish the race with winning status. Winning a race depends on how an athlete orchestrates his step backward and his looking back at this foundational position as preparation for going forward. Some coaches tell their runners to get familiar, even comfortable with the set, start position because if they are only thinking about the sound of the starting gun shot and focusing on the lead hand or leg – then their feet will not be positioned properly to apply force to the blocks in order to have the agility and speed to run the course and finish the race a winner. The foundation affects the smooth execution of the whole race.

Parallel the technique of this natural race with that of the spiritual race we run in Christ. The foundation is of vital importance. To finish the Christian race, we too must take the time to STEP BACK and LOOK BACK as foundation for moving forward. The only way we can grow and go forward is continuing to reflect on Biblical prototypes and foundation given by God to dictate a God inspired future. Often believers have great aspirations and plans to run full throttle ahead, but we forget to step back, look back and see the value of foundational patterns for our lives and the life of the Lord's church. There are so many Biblical patterns that serve as the foundation we must continue to build on today; we must not neglect step back and look at them. This text mentions only a few.

Step Back To Sprint Forward

Dr. Cecilia Jackson

STEP BACK TO SPRINT FORWARD
(God's Biblical Prototypes for Moving Forward Today)

Table of Contents

	Page
Introduction	3
Chapter 1 Preparation for the Challenge	7
Chapter 2 Emerging from the Ashes of Corruption	9
Chapter 3 An Honest Yearning	17
Chapter 4 Follow the Pattern	19
Chapter 5 Prototype "A"–– From Egypt to the Wilderness Church	23
Chapter 6 Prototype "B"––The Holy Spirit Outpouring /Pentecost	27
Chapter 7 Prototype "C"–– Building His Ecclesia	31
Chapter 8 Prototype "D"–– The Rod and The Sword	35
Chapter 9 Prototype "E"––Trumpets, Pitchers, and A Shout/ Gideon	39
Chapter 10 Conclusion	47
Bibliography	49

Step Back To Sprint Forward

Dr. Cecilia Jackson

Chapter 1
Preparation for the Challenge

There have been many moves, transitions, periods of change, and obvious shifts of characteristics of the church as she has developed from one era to the next. Questions being asked in today's church are: How do we prepare for another great explosion of the Spirit of God upon the earth through the church? Will God use His church for the next major spiritual explosion in the earth? The Bible says the harvest is ripe, which means people are in the gateway of expectation for intensification of God's power in the earth; but the laborers are few, which means there is a need for Christians/believers to be prepared to do what is necessary to see a supernatural emergence and augmentation of God's power as was seen in the days of old. So, how do believers and how does the church position itself and ready itself for the upcoming yet present harvest? How does the body of Christ prepare for the enlargement and invasion of God's awesome power upon the earth in this generation to meet the demands of the harvest? What is God's expectation of us? How do we maintain God's earnest heart?

In order to broach this topic, the best method is to look at history and look at the Word of God, the Bible, and see documented patterns of the anointing of God as He transitioned His people in and through major moves in the earth. These patterns highlight principles and principles establish doctrine and set a precedent for expected and anticipated models and standards. What is God's expectation of us? How does the body of Christ prepare for a major move of God in the earth? Go back and study patterns, principles, models and standards; apply those strategies and listen to the voice of the Lord in prayer as He enlightens and breathes on the patterns in history and in His Word in order to walk in the present plan. Step Back to Go Forward.

Dr. Cecilia Jackson

Chapter 2
Emerging from the Ashes of Corruption

We know from study in church history that the church in the Middle Ages had declined to a status of dishonesty and corruption. The clergy was spiritually blind and deaf with regard to sensitivity to God's Spirit. Traditions of men had robbed the church of its due spiritual heritage and had allowed false demands of man to set up false doctrine as a way of life for the people. Superficial bondage had choked the life out of God's people, but God would not leave His church in such a state. He promised to restore all that was lost, even His people's stumbling into rituals that were not the ways of their Godly ancestors. God said He would restore all the locusts and worms had taken from His people.

Jeremiah 18:15 "Because my people hath forgotten me, they have burned incense to vanity, and they have caused them to stumble in their ways from the ancient paths, to walk in paths, in a way not cast up."

Isaiah 58:12 "And they that shall be of thee shall build the old waste places: thou shalt raise up the foundations of many generations; and thou shalt be called, The repairer of the breach, The restorer of paths to dwell in."

Joel 2:25 "And I will restore to you the years that the locust hath eaten, the cankerworm, and the caterpiller, and the palmerworm, my great army which I sent among you."

The level of corruption in the Middle Ages was similar to the condition of the Aaronic priesthood during the time of the judges in Biblical history. The priest of Israel, Eli, was not sensitive to the voice of God and his sons also were immoral (1 Samuel 2).

The scripture states that the true Word of The Lord during those days was rare, scarce because the spiritual leader did not know God's expectation (1 Samuel 3), therefore the people had no vision.

Although things looked dark for the people of God, the Lord would not let it remain that way. He raised up a Samuel, a young man whose pure ministry began a cycle of restoration in Israel.

This parallels what happened during the Middle Ages. The Dark Ages left the church is ruins, but God will never let the lamp of his light of truth go out, so emerging from the ashes of corruption. God called a man named Martin Luther who began his life as a lawyer, but became troubled by certain truths of the church. He gave himself to studying and was one day climbing the steps of St. Peter's Cathedral repeating the Lord's Prayer as an attempt to pray his father out of purgatory, which was a ritual set up by the Roman Catholic Church, when he began to doubt the traditions of the church even more. In his time of crying out to God in prayer and study, he was reading Romans 1:16-17 and the Spirit of God made the truth alive that the just shall live by faith and not by the mere works of man. About the year 1517 Luther began to teach against the established false doctrine in the land and although condemned by the Roman Church, he taught that Christ alone was the only mediator between God and man. He denied the pope and all of the rituals set up by the Roman Catholic Church, thus without planned intent but based on divine inspiration and revelation, the Lutheran Church was founded resulting from separation of many from the Catholic Church.

Following this massive movement, believes began again, to cry out to God in prayer for understanding and truth was revealed to men like Hubmaier and Grebel who established that if baptism is by faith, how could infants receive automatic salvation? Thus before long these believers re-instituted baptism by immersion. Believers began to see the truth regarding water baptism, hence the institution of the Anabaptists, or Baptists began, based on the principles of immersion as a foundation for water baptism. This group became outcasts from the traditional groups of Catholics and Lutherans and they were persecuted by the traditional believers, even to the extent that believers wanting to be baptized were sometimes held under water until they drowned. It is interesting to note that the same ones who were open to progressive truth became the persecutors of it.

As God's people continued to hunger for Him, and seek Him through prayer for answers, God responded by speaking to his people! In the latter part of the 17th Century, men like Whitfield, Zinzendorf and Philipp Spencer began to preach that the Christian life was more than just attending church and rigid doctrinal correctness, but there should be a separation or difference between the lifestyle of believers and that of the world. Holiness became the message of the era! The strongest voice at the time proclaiming holiness was John Wesley. He preached with a new enthusiasm that believers are responsible for how they live and that without holiness no man will see the Lord (Hebrews 14:14). Believers began to live more victorious lives, engage in principles of fasting and prayer, and how to discipline them-selves in their Christian walk. Because the face of church was beginning to change in that Bible study and prayer became vitally important as a method of effective Christian living, this group became known as the Methodists.

Approximately one hundred years later (1844-1919) God, by His Spirit, moved upon a Presbyterian minister, Albert Benjamin Simpson, who through experience in his personal gross loss of health due to overexertion, understood that man was composed of body, soul, and spirit and he became convinced that God was concerned about and had the power to cure both a sick body and a sin sick soul. God restored the truth of Divine healing by healing Simpson extending his life and ministry an additional 35 years. He established the foundation that Jesus Christ is Savior, sanctifier, healer and the coming King who will rule throughout eternity.

God was moving simultaneously throughout the earth where believers were praying, fasting and seeking God for His outpouring! In 1901 in Topeka Kansas a group began to speak in tongues and prophesy and the Welsh revival broke out in 1904-05! This all set the stage for 1906, Los Angeles, when the famous Azusa Street Revivals broke out in America. The Pentecostal movement was ignited! The fires of Pentecost were so intense that this move of God was felt around the world! Previous visitations were seated in the change of the inner man primarily, but as God poured out of His Spirit outward demonstration exuded as men spoke in tongues and prophesied the Word of the Lord! Yes, these believers were persecuted and some were ex-communicated from various churches, but the next move of God had begun!

This explosion of God's purpose was foretold in the scriptures:

Joel 2:26-29 "And ye shall eat in plenty, and be satisfied, and praise the name of the LORD your God, that hath dealt wondrously with you: and my people shall never be ashamed. And ye shall know that I am in the midst of Israel, and that I am the LORD your God, and none else: and my people shall never be ashamed. And it shall come to pass afterward, that I will pour out my spirit upon all flesh; and your sons and your daughters shall prophesy, your old men shall dream dreams, your young men shall see visions: And also upon the servants and upon the handmaids in those days will I pour out my spirit."

Acts 2:16-18 "But this is that which was spoken by the prophet Joel; And it shall come to pass in the last days, saith God, I will pour out of my Spirit upon all flesh: and your sons and your daughters shall prophesy, and your young men shall see visions, and your old men shall dream dreams:

Dr. Cecilia Jackson

And on my servants and on my handmaidens I will pour out in those days of my Spirit; and they shall prophesy."

The root of the new resurgence of the gifts of the spirit in the 1970's goes back to 1900, movement-- the most widely accepted date for what is now known as the classical Pentecostal movement. During a watch night service beginning on December 31, 1900, and ending on what is technically the first day of the twentieth century, Charles Parham of Topeka, Kansas, laid his hands on Agnes Ozman and she began speaking in tongues. Thus, the movement began. A sweeping, spectacular chain of experiences led to the famous Los Angeles Azusa Street Revival, which began in 1906 under the ministry of William Seymour. With that revitalization which spread nationwide, the Pentecostal movement gained high attention, respect, and momentum. This energy has never slackened.

The original intent of Pentecostal leaders was to influence the major Christian denominations. But as we look at church history from Martin Luther, John Wesley, Lutheranism and its incompatible doctrine to the Catholic Church in the sixteenth century, the Methodist and its incompatible doctrine with the Anglican Church in the eighteenth century; Pentecostalism found itself incompatible with the mainline doctrine of American churches in the early twentieth century. Thus, as others had done before them, Pentecostal leaders reluctantly found it necessary to form new denominations where they could practice a Christian lifestyle directly under the influence of the Holy Spirit. We know today of these denominations as: Assemblies of God, Pentecostal Holiness, Church of God in Christ, Church of the Foursquare Gospel, Church of God, Church of the Living God, Apostolic Holiness, Fire Baptized and others were formed for that purpose.

In 1960, Dennis Bennett, an Episcopal priest in Van Nuys, California, explained to his congregation that he had received the Holy Spirit in the Pentecostal way (which meant speaking in tongues). This marked what became known as the Charismatic Movement! The Charismatic Movement took form first as renewal movements within major existing denominations such as Catholics, Methodists, Episcopalians, and Presbyterians. Then around 1970, the independent Charismatic Movement began with the emergence of free-standing charismatic churches, separate from established denominations, and they took on a new momentum: New Testament Churches, Non-Denominational churches with names including scriptural references like rock, harvest, "church" and "ministries" instead of; "temple" "chapel", dropping denominational handles such as Baptist, Holiness, Pentecostal, and Apostolic. A newly born type of church was formed and swept through the nation. For the next 30 years, these independent charismatic churches were the fastest-growing group of churches in the United States.

The broader distinguishing feature of these new movements was not just tongues, but rather the whole biblical dynamics of the operation of spiritual gifts in a new and exciting way, and the recognition of the need for the 5-fold ministry gifts in the Body of Christ. Through their discovery of how the gifts of the Spirit were intended to operate in the Body of Christ, the Holy Spirit began and is now being transformed from abstract doctrine written in books and explored in the minds of theologians, to dynamic experiences prevalent and functioning in order and effectively in the Body of Christ.

With the upsurge and awakening of the Baptism of the Holy Spirit, there naturally comes a stirring and rejuvenated emphasis on the gifts, the fruit of the Spirit, and the 5-fold ministries of the church. The fruit of the Spirit is worked in the believer through the gradual process of life's experiences, but the gifts of God are given as it pleases God by his grace. There are different kinds of gifts, but it is God's Spirit that works them all for the purpose of profiting the body of Christ. This is also the case for the ministries or offices in the body of Christ.

The move of the Baptism in the Holy Spirit also ushered in the doctrine of the Laying on of Hands, the Revelation of the Body of Christ, the ascension gift ministries, principles of church order and government, worship in Spirit and in

Dr. Cecilia Jackson

truth, and the maturity of the saints, including the restoration of the offices of the prophets and the apostles.

Reading 1 Corinthians, chapter 12; Hebrews 6:1-2; Acts 28:8; 1 Timothy 4:14; Ephesians 5:27; Ephesians 1:22-23; Ephesians 4:8-11; and other reference scriptures will be helpful in establishing Biblical support for the authenticity of the historical moves as they parallel God's unfolding plan for His people.

These historical moves Emerging from the Ashes of Corruption of the churches during the Dark Ages/Middle Ages, set the foundation for the progressive moves of God in the earth and He continues to visit His people and move them forward in His purpose for these times.

Even decades since the world wide impact of the Baptism of the Holy Spirit, in our life time many of us have seen and some have even been a part of the birth of the moves of God that have emerged from the Pentecostal move and the baptism of the Holy Spirit such as: Presbytery and the Laying on of Hands, miracles and healings attached to an upsurge of tent revivals, healing revivals as attached to Oral Roberts University, the Word of Faith Movement as associated with Kenneth Hegan and Rhema, the Prosperity Movement as associated with Kenneth Copeland and minister Creflo Dollar, the Intellectual Business Movement of men and women as associated with the Assemblies of God, the Leadership and Fathering awakening as associated with Dr, Mark Hanby, the Teaching Explosion as associated with Bible Temple University, the revelation of The Church and the Gifts as associated with Dr. Bill Hammon, the Movement of Intercessory Prayer, the Purpose and Destiny Movement as associated with Miles Monroe, the Deliverance Movement -- casting out devils, the movement of Evangelism and Servant Evangelism in the community as characterized by the Vineyard and several other major names, and the Movement of the restoration of the Apostles and Prophets. Of course, this is merely a brief list.

The current, crucial, earnest questions being asked now are: So, how do believers and how does the church position itself and ready itself for the upcoming yet present harvest? How does the body of Christ prepare for the enlargement and invasion of God's awesome power upon the earth in this generation to meet the demands of the harvest? What is God's expectation of us now? How do we know God's earnest heart for today?

Dr. Cecilia Jackson

Chapter 3
An Honest Yearning

Some individuals by the divine hand of God were placed from eternity, before birth, into a generation that actually lived to see some of the major changes in the moves of God on the earth since the Baptism in the Holy Spirit and the Pentecostal Movement. They and millions like them have an Honest Yearning to move and flow with God's purpose as did the patriarchs in world history and Biblical history. They do not want to be numb and asleep to God's present and proceeding voice, but they want to be awake and alert to every word that proceeds out of the mouth of God.

As children they have peeked through the sticks and steaks of tents where revivals were held in open air on vacant inner-city street lots where God's people cried out hungry for miracles, signs, and wonders in the earth. They saw God moving in great healings and miracles and deliverance. What they saw drew them to the front rows in these places of sawdust and anointed oil cloths and nail pegs because their hearts desired God and all He was.

As teens some of them (in Cincinnati, Ohio) flocked to Uptown Revival Center and W.E.B. Grant to see God move powerfully in the gifts of the Word of Wisdom and Knowledge and Faith and Miracles. Some walked through and participated in the holiness movement – the most effective times of Fire Baptized Churches founded on teachings of believers being filled with the Holy Ghost, fire, faith and living holy lives that supported healings and miracles.

As young adults some of them were still being birthed as they let their hunger attach it's arms around the move of the full Gospel Business Assemblies and Aglow fellowships being born and the power and Spirit of God invading the sophisticated carnal minds of the more wealthy citizens of our land. It was no longer miracles and wonders and healings only for the poor who had only God as hope[17] because they did not have enough money to sustain them. The affluent were impacted and their pride disarmed because God moved mightily by His Spirit and the spirit of God fell upon believers in the Catholic churches producing tongue talking nuns and priests who left the priesthood and convents to receive Christ in a new and more powerful way.

The believers who experienced these transitions are very earnest and committed to obeying the voice of The Lord for today wherever He may be speaking for them to go, and whatever He may be speaking for them to say. I am blessed to be a believer who was birthed and grew up in and through some of these awe-inspiring, extraordinary, yet humbling moves of God, thus I and other friends in the ministry like me, have a common cry before the Lord today, "Please don't pass me by. I want to be a part of the purpose of God for this generation, this era".

They and millions like them have an Honest Yearning to move and flow with God's purpose as did the patriarchs in world history and Biblical history. Surely there IS a way to follow God and be in harmony, in accord, and synchronized with His voice and His plan.

Chapter 4
Follow the Pattern

How do we prepare for another great explosion of the Spirit of God upon the earth through the church? The Bible says the harvest is ripe, which means people are in the gateway of expectation for intensification of God's power in the earth; but the laborers are few, which means there is a need for Christians/believers to be prepared to do what is necessary to see a supernatural emergence and augmentation of God's power as was seen in the days of old. So, how do believers and how does the church position itself and ready itself for the upcoming yet present harvest? How does the body of Christ prepare for the enlargement and invasion of God's awesome power upon the earth in this generation to meet the demands of the harvest? What is God's expectation of us? How do we execute God's earnest heart in the matters of today? The answer is simply: Follow the Pattern, Look Back to Go forward!

The answer to these questions is quite simple: Follow the Pattern. Stick to the principles. There are patterns, principles, and examples God used throughout Biblical history and these patterns have echoed throughout the generations how He moves, His character, His principles, His heart concerning His plan, and what atmosphere is present when His approval is with His creation – man! Look Back to Sprint Forward.

We are living in a time of: advanced sociological development and studies, advanced medical, technological, environmental development and studies; advanced educational pursuit, psychological, biological, chemical, and physiological study and pursuit, and every other kind of advanced study that can be concocted in the mind of man. Because of this chase for something different, something new, something unusual, and atypical -- leaders are looking for something extraordinary to preach to their people and people are running from meeting to meeting looking for some outlandish, weird and wonderful truth that is "deep" and mystical.

How sad is the day in these times when while this debauchery is going on, God is saying He already has a pattern, a way, and a plan. Nothing is more extraordinary than what is already documented in the Word of God. Some of the most profound words that God has said to man throughout Biblical scripture have been, "see that you do it according to the pattern". He knew there would come a time where men would have "itching ears" and want to create something of their own wisdom and their own Babel, so He advised thousands of years ago to do whatever you do for Him, seeking Him, and unto Him "according to the pattern", according to what He has already laid out for you to do. A pattern is an example, a blueprint, an outline or prototype, a guide a sample. It is a mold, copy, design, or precedent by which something is to be followed.

The subsequent chapters are a few Biblical examples of patterns and prototypes we can follow today that prepare us to remain in the flow of God's preparation as He is walking us through a supernatural emergence and augmentation of His power as was seen in the days of old; and as He is walking us through the gateway of intensification of God's power in the earth doing the "greater works we will do" that are necessary for receiving and equipping for today's harvest.

Keep these truths in mind:

1) It is God's magnificence and splendor to cover some matters and advice from us as a challenge for us to seek to learn about Him. But it should be our honor as the royal sons and daughters of God to search, examine and study His truths, His ways, and His character so that we will be motivated to take action and do His will which is in His Word.

<u>Proverbs 25:2</u> "It is the glory (splendor, magnificence) of God to conceal (saw – thar' –cover, hide in secret) a thing: (daw – bawr' – a Word, advice, matter) but the honour of kings (meh' -lek – royalty) such as we are is to search out a matter (examine it, penetrate it – that is motivate the matter and stir it up, and give motion/action to it)."

2) The things that occurred in Biblical history happened for our patterns and examples of approval (what to do) or (disapproval) what to avoid doing.

1 Corinthians 10:11 "Now all these things happened unto them for ensamples (sample & patterns): and they are written for our admonition, (calling attention to upon whom the ends of the world are come)."

3) Jesus declared that the entire Bible was written about things related to Him. This includes things related to Him and the Church from beginning to end – pre-existence, existence, throughout eternity.

Hebrews 10:7 "Then said I (Jesus), Lo, I come (in the volume of the book it is written of me,) to do thy will, O God."

Romans 15:4 "For whatsoever things were written aforetime were written for our learning, that we through patience and comfort of the scriptures might have hope."

4) The Lord is God who does not change. People change, laws and governments change, society changes, situations change; however, the Lord is constant and sturdy. He, nor His Word, changes. So we are going to the scriptures for the examples, patterns, guides and designs for comfort and hope in knowing "He will do it Again"!! Yes, there were many major moves of God throughout history, both natural and Biblical, but the same ingredients in those patterns are the ones God will use today! We must Follow the Prototypes and Step Back, Look Back then Go Forward!

Malachi 3:6 "For I am the LORD, I change not!"

Step Back To Sprint Forward

Dr. Cecilia Jackson

Chapter 5
Prototype "A"– From Egypt to the Wilderness Church

The move from Egypt to the church in the Wilderness was a major move for God's people. God wanted to have encounters with his people when they left Egypt in obedience to His command. Even the wilderness experience was preparation for the promises of God and continued relationship with God. This precipitated the visitation or the Revival that was to come to the people once they were out of Egypt. A prerequisite for the Revival was the wilderness experience!!

Notice the prefix "PRE", which means "occurring before". Before they could see the more in-depth picture of what God had for them, the followers of God had to begin their walk through the wilderness. By simple definition, a wilderness is a dry, rough wasteland which is inhospitable and harsh. It is considered as badland and desert waste, which means it is desolate, arid and a barren place. God led this people THROUGH this kind of place as the first steps on the path to a more intricate relationship with Him. In fact, He established a plan for them and gave it to Moses while they were on this boondocks of a rough path! Lesson to learn - God will meet you in the roughest, most difficult places of your life when it may seem like you're just in an arid, useless, dry, and hopeless place. Always remember that just as God gave His people a plan in the wilderness in the days of old, He has a plan for you in your wilderness. Do you want to know what God is doing next? You will most likely find yourself if a place where things seen like the most difficult, trying time in your life, but God IS there and will give you water in your wilderness. He has a word of direction and instruction that will take you to the next level!

When the people left Egyptian slavery, God gave Moses the plan for His sanctuary while he was in the Mountain (see Exodus 25 – 40). This was not only the plan for "The Church in the Wilderness", but it was a pattern for

Step Back To Sprint Forward

National (natural) Israel and a type and shadow of the New Testament Church Today – which is us – Spiritual Israel. Read your Bible (Rom. #9 and 11, I Cor. #15, Gal. #3 and 6). God wanted a place to live, dwell, meet with His people. God dwelled first WITH men, then among men, and finally IN men! These are words of placement. They are prepositions – words of location! He is with, among, and around, above, through, and upon His creation. Today especially, He lives also IN us in this era; we are above all most blessed! At the same time, we have the most access to the awesome God, Jehovah, Elohim, Emmanuel!

At that time there were at the threshhold of this major move components that aligned His people with His positioning that brought the pillar of cloud by day and fire by night – the Shekinah glory and anointing of God among Israel that ushered in a new thing – another move of God. Lesson to Learn -- The SAME ingredients given to Israel then (that ignited revival for them) Now for us also ignite revival -- visitations from The Lord that produce miracles, signs, wonders, deliverance, changed lives, healing for the broken hearted, unity of the believers that bring in and equip a waiting harvest, and cause to fall upon us blessings that run and catch us and over take us -- Revival -- hallelujah!!

<u>Exodus 35:21-22</u> "And they came, every one whose heart stirred him up, and every one whom his spirit made willing, and they brought the LORD'S offering to the work of the tabernacle of the congregation. And they came, both men and women, as many as were willing hearted, and brought bracelets, and earrings, and rings, and tablets, all jewels of gold: and every man that offered offered an offering of gold unto the LORD."

Lesson to learn - The people were stirred in their hearts and their spirits were willing! Change, a new move, cannot come on the wings of the realm of the soul. It's not an intellectual move that we figure out in our minds reasoning and intelligence. It is certainly not based on our emotions which can change based on any given situation. It requires the "pneuma" (spirit – breath of God) to breathe on us and stir our hearts and spirits to long and pant for God. This kind of revival bypasses the realm of the mind and has to be birthed in one's spirit. The People were stirred in their hearts and in their spirits and were willing to change. They were not resistant to going forward to another place, something they had not seen before, something they had to walk with god in by faith. It was the next move of God for Israel! We are to have the same attitude for what God is endeavoring to do with His church. There has to be an excitement, an anticipation, an enthusiasm, an exhilaration, a stimulation and fervor, an eagerness and a true passion – a heart and spirit that is stirred up and willing to commit to going forward with The Lord! In order for a local church to move forward and transition from an old to a new move with God, the people have to be stirred, motivated and inspired to move forward. When growing in personal vision, the same requirement must be met. It is a foundational requirement.

The Bible says both men and women brought the offerings, gifts, talents, abilities, callings, and were willing to use them in the sanctuary for the glory of God! Not only was this an example of spiritual and natural gifts of God being brought, it was certainly a principle establishing the need for believers to financially invest in the work of the Kingdom with their increase, money, and valuable possessions. Lesson to learn -- Giving is always a prerequisite for receiving. If we want to experience the outpouring of God like never before, we must give like never before – hallelujah!! Bring your tithes and offerings into the store house so there is supply in my house to do the work of harvesting souls for the kingdom and refreshing and revival for those who are already standing and serving in the house of the Lord. We cannot produce care and spiritual nutrition for the harvest if we yourselves are not refreshed! So, have a willing heart and spirit stirred for Kingdom work, and bringing an offering that supports the financial demands of the work!!

What does it look like – a stirred and willing heart loaded with an offering? How can one envision these requirements in the church of God today?

The sound of rejoicing is heard in the camp (saints giving god glory)) The sound of them that say "Amen" (supporting the Word of The Lord) The sound of war being made in the heavenlies (intercession) The sound of the sacrifices of thanksgiving and praise (worship).

Exodus 35:21,26, 36:2 states change occurred by a people stirred up, "whose heart stirred him up....whom his spirit made him willing". Your spirit makes your soul willing. You must be the one to take control of your intellect, your mind, your thoughts and emotions; and order them to be willing according to what God and His Word has dictated. We have to take responsibility to obey God. God will not coerce us. We are made willing by our regenerated spirit, when we think of the awesome goodness of God and all He has done for us in our past. This causes our spirits to trust him and our soul to be made willing to trust him for our future,

The lessons to learn in this chapter were prototypes of the Old Testament Scriptures that were patterns set for our example today. Review each of the four lessons. They were pedestals and foundations for a transition and move of God that functioned for nearly 400 years for the entire nation of Israel. These principles must have been important and functional: typically of the Lord Jesus Christ, prophetically as the local and universal Church of today, dispensationally as appropriate for the ages of times to come, and practically and experientially as they can be applied for inspiring change, growth, and an impelling thrust forward for you and your local church today.

Chapter 6
Prototype "B"– The Holy Spirit Outpouring /Pentecost

The outpouring of the Holy Spirit on the Day of Pentecost was another major transition or major move in the history of God's Kingdom work. What was the pattern, blueprint, sample, or guide that was used then, that we can mark as a prototype for us to model after today? What happened at "Pentecost" that we should mark today?

What occurred on the day of Pentecost as recorded in Acts chapter 2, was the first fulfillment of what the prophets foretold in the Old Testament. In Acts 2:16, Peter states the experience at Pentecost is that which was spoken about by the prophet Joel. He further said these events at Pentecost were the promise of the Father and as Jesus stated, "The promise of the Spirit". He concluded in verses 38 and 39 that the promise of the outpouring they experienced was for them, their children, and as many as the Lord called. We are those God has called for this experience!

Acts 2:16-18 "But this is that which was spoken by the prophet Joel; And it shall come to pass in the last days, saith God, I will pour out of my Spirit upon all flesh: and your sons and your daughters shall prophesy, and your young men shall see visions, and your old men shall dream dreams: And on my servants and on my handmaidens I will pour out in those days of my Spirit; and they shall prophesy."

Lesson to learn - Biblical history and the manners and customs of the Old and New Testament tells us the night before Pentecost morning, the disciples brought offerings to the temple to thank God for His provisions for them. They thanked God for what He had done for them and they sang praises for the blessings of the past, expecting and thanking God in faith, that there would be more blessings to come! They had a praise party the night before Pentecost morning!! The spirit of thanksgiving, praise, and giving in these followers was preparation for the outpouring of the Holy Spirit the next morning at Pentecost! This was the preparation for the next transition in God, the next move of God?

On the evening before the day of Pentecost there was celebration by praise and giving! The Israelites would express their praise and giving hearts by bringing almost every kind of offering imaginable: grain offerings, drink offerings, sin offerings, burnt offerings and freewill offerings establishing a massive spirit of giving. Their hearts were open for a mighty move of God that would change history and usher in a new dimension in knowing God in the Spirit! Their thanksgiving, giving, and praise positioned them to receive from the open heavens of the Lord!

Likewise, we today can expect God to give to us the massive outpouring of the Holy Spirit when we prepare our hearts through massive giving, thanksgiving, and praise! These acts of love to God create God's response which is, He opens the heavens and pours out blessings upon His believers! One of those blessings is the pouring of the Holy Spirit, also known as the baptism in the Holy Spirit or Holy Ghost.

This is why it is easier for believers to receive the baptism in the Holy Spirit during the praise and worship service or some small group gathering of praise, thanksgiving, and giving; because the perfect atmosphere has been created after persons have given of themselves in praising and thanking God for all His goodness to them; and the heavens are thus opened to them to receive from the Lord! Lesson to learn -- Praise, thanksgiving, and giving are prerequisites to moving forward and receiving from The Lord!

When Israel left Egypt they did not go directly into the Promised Land. God led them to Mount Horeb which was also called Mount Sinai. Exactly fifty days after the Passover from Egypt, God called Moses to the top of Mount Sinai and there the heavens opened and God gave him the law, more historically accurate, He gave them the Torah or the teachings of God. This was the revelation of God's will for man to live by. It revealed God's love for man and His character towards man. This was the first 5 books of the Bible.

Lesson to learn -- During the time Jesus lived, part of the celebration of Pentecost also included staying up all night studying God's Word! It was a way of studying His word afresh!

What would they have studied? Any devout Jew would have been aware of the promise of the outpouring of the Holy Spirit. They studied the scrolls of God's blessings to their forefathers; these were pages from the Torah. Would they have studied the promises of Joel about the day when all would receive the Spirit of God? Or would they read Ezekiel's vision about the Lord coming in a whirlwind with flames of fire? Would they have studied the words in the Torah received by Moses? Yes, is the answer to all those questions!

Lesson to learn -- When Pentecost morning dawned, they were all gathered there in the Upper Room. They were already there because they had stayed all night celebrating, giving thanks, praising, and reading the Word of God! These were actions, proceedings, measures taken that ushered in, escorted in a major move or transition in Biblical history of God's plan for man!

We thank him with our giving of monetary offerings, our giving Him words of adoration, our words of appreciation, words that magnify Him, words that ascribe to Him honor and glory. We spend time reading His precious Word. He sees and hears our efforts of love displayed to Him and is pleased. Then He opens the heavens and pours out blessings upon us. He directs our path. We receive all we need to live a victorious life: health, provision, healings, working of wonders and miracles, peace, joy, and also the outpouring of His Holy Spirit to abide with us as an advocate forever! These were behaviors, actions that set the stage for a deeper move of God's presence on the earth in His people.

Then when the day of Pentecost had fully come, they were in the Upper Room unified in their thinking and the heavens were torn, rend open (from the Greek word schizo) and the power of God was released into the earth realm! As the fire came down and the Glory of God on Sinai, the fire and the Glory of God came down upon His disciples! The result -- a new, transitional move of God -- the Holy Spirit Baptism upon all who were in the room; the result, they spoke with tongues! (Read Acts Chapter 2. Also, see my book: PPT -- Passover, Pentecost and Trumpets for details about Pentecost)

Let's simply follow the Pattern. Stick to the principles. There are patterns, principles, and examples God used throughout Biblical history and these patterns have echoed throughout the generations telling how He moves, His character, His principles, His heart concerning His plan, and what atmosphere is present when His approval is with His creation. Let's mimic the prototype, follow the pattern and walk into the revelation of what is proceeding out of the heart and mouth of God for today for us! Look Back, then Go Forward!

Chapter 7
Prototype "C"-- Building His Ecclesia

Things are accelerating in the earth and we are on the entry level stages of His GLORY invading the earth!! These are amazing times!! When God is moving in His Glory, it doesn't matter who the president is, who the generals are, who is in earthly office because God sweeps in and invades through His people through His government. When His government is functioning properly through His Ecclesia CHANGE occurs that the government of man cannot hold back nor contain!! How do we propel change, transition today? Follow the pattern of His Ecclesia, His government, and remember the rod and the sword.

The components of His Ecclesia are simply: people, dedication, consecration, and sacrifice.

Matthew 16:13-18 "When Jesus came into the coasts of Caesarea Philippi, he asked his disciples, saying, Whom do men say that I the Son of man am? And they said, Some say that thou art John the Baptist: some, Elias; and others, Jeremias, or one of the prophets. He saith unto them, But whom say ye that I am? And Simon Peter answered and said, Thou art the Christ, the Son of the living God. And Jesus answered and said unto him, Blessed art thou, Simon Barjona: for flesh and blood hath not revealed it unto thee, but my Father which is in heaven. And I say also unto thee, That thou art Peter, and upon this rock I will build my church; and the gates of hell shall not prevail against it."

Let's take a look at a brief breakdown of the key words in verses 16 – 18 of Mathew's gospel.

Spiritual stone (rock) Build Meaning: to be a house builder, construct (figuratively) confirm: - (be in) build, edify, embolden, bolster, erect, put together, and to assemble.

MY church ek-klay-see'-ah – (Greek) Meaning: a calling out, that is, (concretely) a popular meeting, especially a religious congregation, Christian community of members on earth or saints in heaven or both): - assembly, church.

According to history in Biblical days, the "Ek-klay-see'-ah" was begun by the Romans. When the Roman soldiers went into a territory and victoriously took over, the first thing they did in the conquered city was set up the "ecclesia" to establish the Roman government in the new land – in that newly conquered city. The role of the ecclesia was to make the city an exact replica of Rome in every aspect. It was to mirror Rome in all forms. For example: Roman Government, education, financial systems and currency, entertainment, clothing, culture, language, trends, morals and conduct, everything!!

That's why Jesus said I will build MY ecclesia!! The church is to model His government, education, financial system, culture, morals, standards, language, clothing, conduct, everything!! All aspects of one's life are to be God-centered. Lesson to learn -- Just as the Romans came in and changed, adjusted lifestyle and values, Christ desires to come in and impact our lives in every way. He wants to tear down other forms of government and set up His Ecclesia, His total government, in our lives and churches. And scripture declares the gates of hell, the troubles and threats of satan's plans, no storm we encounter in life can dominate nor win against us, His church, His people. A prototype or Biblical pattern for moving forward in the center of God's plan is to allow Him to build your life, His Ecclesia, His church.

Concluding:

- His ecclesia moves the ministry of the kingdom forward.

- They are DOERS and not just HEARERS of the word.

- Like some of the children of Israel, they did not want to continue to wander another 40 years in the wilderness; they were more interested in going on with God and being a wonder instead of wandering.

Look Back at this patters, and Go Forward in God's Kingdom work!

Dr. Cecilia Jackson

Chapter 8
Prototype "D"– The Rod and The Sword

So, how do believers and how does the church position itself and ready itself for the upcoming yet present harvest? How does the body of Christ prepare for the enlargement and invasion of God's awesome power upon the earth in this generation and prepare to meet the demands of the harvest? What is God's expectation of us? How do we maintain God's earnest heart? I believe the best approach is to look at history and look at the Word of God, the Bible, and see documented patterns of the anointing of God as He transitioned His people in and through major moves in the earth.

One of most important documented incidents that sets a prototype and pattern for us today, is portions of the narrative of Moses and Joshua. Lesson to learn -- I tenaciously believe to be empowered to go to the next level of the Ecclesia that God is anointing in this era, we must have the kind of unity that tightly binds the Rod and the Sword – the old men and the young men!

Joe 2:27 And ye shall know that I am in the midst of Israel, and that I am the LORD your God, and none else: and my people shall never be ashamed. Joe 2:28 And it shall come to pass afterward, that I will pour out my spirit upon all flesh; and your sons and your daughters shall prophesy, your old men shall dream dreams, your young men shall see visions:

Lesson to learn -- In order to see acceleration and a great degree of the miraculous in churches in America today, there must be a working together, a blending of those two generations mentioned in Joel. This is one of the foundations that must be laid for the end-time revival in America to break out with the unrestrained power of God —a blending of the two generations – the old and young – the rod and the sword!

Step Back To Sprint Forward

When the ROD of Moses (which represents authority with God, insight, wisdom, and understanding) blends with the SWORD of Joshua (which represents skill, strength and militaristic strategy), we will see the wheels of revival turn in a more profound and exacting manner that will paralyze the enemy and produce a more glorious church taking captive a ready harvest!

Lesson to learn -- The seamless merging of these two will establish common cause and a UNITY in the Ecclesia, which will provide the pedestal for miracles and signs and wonders and above all else, the influx of the greatest harvest the new world has known in AMERICA!! There must be a blending and a unifying and proper positioning and – strategy with the voice of ONE -- then the SOUND from Zion will produce a praise and power that will reek havoc, chaos, bedlam, turmoil, madness, and mayhem in the camp of satan breaking the cords of the wicked in the land! There must be the two working together – the old and the young!!

Sometimes the growing process causes static, frustration, criticism, disappointments, and even offense at leadership meetings; but the great God is in the midst to bring together the two for the new stage of transition for the church! The results are worth the process required to get to the symphony between the old and the young – the rod and the sword.

If revival only comes through the sword of Joshua, it will not last and the waters will dry soon thereafter. Neither will revival come with Moses alone. There must be the ROD and the SWORD! Hallelujah!!

Exodus 17 paraphrased states that when Israel left Egypt, they took most of the Egyptians goods and this provoked surrounding nations. Moses told Joshua to select some warriors to fight against the enemy. As Joshua and his men fought (skill, strength, strategy) -- Moses stood at the top of the hill with his arms stretched – holding tight to his Rod (authority with God, wisdom, insight, understanding).

Lesson to learn -- As long as Moses stood gripping the Rod, Joshua prevailed in battle – the army excelled and the enemy was defeated. The moment Moses' arms grew tired from his position of authority, the army weakened and the enemy began to lose effect in battle. When Moses' arms grew tired of carrying the weight of the authority and his responsibility for wisdom and understanding as the leader upholding the rod –- there arose a problem. Lesson to learn --Joshua's victory was dependent upon Moses being in POSIION with the rod of God. No matter how skilled Joshua was as a warrior, the skill and ability was functional only with Moses' rod as a covering. No matter how wise and understanding Moses was of the mind of God and the insight he had which further plugged him into the authority of God, he still needed the skill, strength and strategies of Joshua and his men in order to defeat the enemy.   It was designed by God as a unity factor necessary for going forward and defeating the enemy.

The things in the old pattern were done for us as an example. To be empowered to go to the next level of the Ecclesia that God is anointing in this era, we must have the kind of unity that tightly binds the Rod and the Sword – the old men and the young men!

Step Back To Sprint Forward

Dr. Cecilia Jackson

Chapter 9
Prototype "E"– Trumpets, Pitchers, and A Shout/ Gideon

The final and very important Biblical pattern this book addresses is the fact that God determines His strategy for progression and victory. It is not a requirement to have large numbers of members in a congregation or many followers on a team that is on a mission for Christ. Lesson to learn -- Great numbers is not a prerequisite; Gideon followed God's instructions and won one of the greatest battles in Biblical history with trumpets, pitchers and exuberant, fierce shouts from his army! The greatest need: get God's mind on the matter, get His instructions. If God gives you instructions and you follow them, a small group can accomplish a great task.

Just before the children of Israel entered Canaan, they won a pounding victory over the Midianites (Num. 31: 1-18) and the Midianites had ever since been sore enemies against Israel. After some time, they felt strong enough to attack Israel in revenge and was planning to do so.

The Midianites conducted warfare differently than other nations. They did not administer organized rule or government over countries; instead, they were desert people whose custom was to make periodic disparaging raids on the people who cultivated their soil. They would allow the people to plant and reap the harvest of their crop; but when the harvest was successfully brought in, they would raid, invade, rob and take the fruit of their labor.

When the children of Israel were in distress, they would always cry to the Lord and He would send a prophet to tell them why they were in trouble and God, because of His mercy, would work out a way to deliver His people.

At this time a man named Gideon of the tribe of Manasseh was separating his grain from the stalks, but was hiding beside a winepress which is a piece of winemaking equipment that squeezes the juice from grapes. He was harvesting his grain in secrecy because the Midianites would find the fruit of his labor and take it. The situation was so serious that many of God's people had fled to live in caves and dens in the mountains (Judges 6:2).

One day when Gideon was working with his wheat, a strange man appeared carrying a staff of sorts in his hand. Gideon greeted the stranger and the man told him the Lord was with him and called him a mighty man of valor (Judges 6:12). Gideon was surprised and responded that if God was with him, then where are the miracles and wonders that their forefathers experienced? Furthermore, he questioned that God had left then and given them to the Midianites to destroy (Judges 6:13).

These thoughts parallel the thoughts of some believers today who ask: Since we are supposed to be doing greater works than in the times of old, where are the miracles? When will there be a move of God on the earth that will cause signs, wonders, miracles and deliverance as was seen by our spiritual forefathers? If God is with us, where are the miracles the scripture says we should be doing? Either Christ cannot perform them in our times, or we are missing some great facts concerning what we are doing that is prohibiting a great move of God. We know the latter part of the statement is true – we are missing some things we should be doing to cause the desired results. The problem is not God's ability, nor his desire to help us! Gideon's mistake was he failed to place the blame where it belonged – on the children of Israel.

Lesson to learn -- God is raising up men and women who have disproved the fiction that the days of miracles are over and the move of God in signs and wonders and power is a thing of the past. Jesus Christ is the same yesterday, today, and forever (Hebrews 13:8). God does not change; man does. We are seeing and will see ministry of the supernatural, unprecedented since the days of the Early Church.

Gideon asked the question, "If the Lord is with us why is all this misfortune happening to us; why aren't se seeing the miracles?" Instead of answering the question, the angel gave Gideon a command to go in his might and that he would save Israel because God was sending him to do the work. Gideon told the angel of his weakness, his inability and the poverty of his people of Manasseh. Gideon asked for a sign from God to prove that the command was true.

<u>Judges 6:14-17</u> "And the LORD looked upon him, and said, Go in this thy might, and thou shalt save Israel from the hand of the Midianites: have not I sent thee? And he said unto him, Oh my Lord, wherewith shall I save Israel? behold, my family is poor in Manasseh, and I am the least in my father's house. And the LORD said unto him, Surely I will be with thee, and thou shalt smite the Midianites as one man. And he said unto him, If now I have found grace in thy sight, then shew me a sign that thou talkest with me."

Gideon's reaction was similar to that of Moses at the Burning Bush. He began to make excuses. His family lived in the area where the Midianites frequently raided Israel, which is confirmed by his hiding behind the wine pressing machinery in order to not be seen by his oppressor. The family needed the harvest in order to be feed and have other basic needs met. The Lord gave Gideon almost the same message He gave Moses; He would be with him and would destroy the enemy as one (Judges 6:16).

Perhaps Gideon wanted to strengthen his faith by asking the heavenly messenger for a sign. He brought a goat and some flour to the angel who was under an oak tree. The angel told Gideon to pour the flour out and put the goat on a rock. As he touched the flesh of the goat with his staff, a flame of fire burst out of the rock and burnt up the entire sacrifice; then the angel vanished. Gideon then knew for certain this was God's messenger and that God would be with him. It was said in those days that if someone saw an angel, he would die (Jud. 13:22). Therefore, The Lord took time to assure Gideon that this superstition would have no effect on him by declaring peace upon his life and commanding him not to fear because he would not die. Lesson to learn - When God calls one to go forward in Him, He is concerned about, and will attend to even his or her smallest concerns.

Judges 6:22-24 "And when Gideon perceived that he was an angel of the LORD, Gideon said, Alas, O Lord GOD! for because I have seen an angel of the LORD face to face. And the LORD said unto him, Peace be unto thee; fear not: thou shalt not die. Then Gideon built an altar there unto the LORD, and called it Jehovahshalom: unto this day it is yet in Ophrah."

Gideon was told next, to take his father's bull that was left from the family's heard and to prepare it for sacrifice on the altar where the shrine of Baal stood. Gideon was also told to cut down the trees surrounding Baal's altar. This was a terrifying task, but Gideon did it. No one was brave enough to destroy the shrines of Baal, especially during a time when the Midianites had such a strong arm on the neck of Israel. The Bible says Gideon was fearful to destroy the altars during the day, but he did it at night. Lesson to learn – One could say that Gideon was cowardly because he did the job at night, but the important thing to remember is that he did it. With 10 trusted men, he accomplished the task under the cover of the night. He obeyed the command of God to him. One will never see a move of God even today, unless obedience is a foundational commitment.

Eventually Gideon was under suspicion for destroying the altars of Baal and other men in the city vowed vengeance against him. It was Joash, Gideon's father, who came to his defense as he was becoming more convinced that Baal was powerless (Judges 6:31). Although Joash had erected the altar of Baal, it appears that he had lost faith in Baal. Gideon had gained an ally in the one he thought would be most angry with him. Therefore, he sent a call throughout Manasseh and the surrounding tribes for help for battle and received an enthusiastic response.

Gideon's army grew to a total of 32,000 men, while the Midianites numbered 150,000 men. It seemed this number would be too small to fight the Midianites, but God told Gideon that his army was too large and that he must reduce it because the people must know that the battle will be won by God and not by the hands of man. Lesson to learn -- God's plan for a miraculous demonstration of power does not have to be with mass numbers of people. He will move in power in this era with not only large congregations, but God will move with those who are the mighty few to trust and obey Him!

God further instructed Gideon to release the men who were fearful, which reduced the army by some 22,000 (after they saw the size of the Midianite army). Lesson to learn – When going forward in the plan and purpose for God in this era, faith is a prerequisite rather than fear. Those who will move with God must be convinced that no matter how things look, greater is the Lord who is for us than those who are against us. The 22,000 men who were fearful saw that the enemy was 6 times greater than they, so they felt (naturally) they did not stand a chance. Trying to go forward with those who are full of fear will be a burden. It's much better that they depart the battle. When this happens, the focus will be on expecting the supernatural power of God to do what He declared He would do.

Gideon released the fearful with honor. Lesson to learn -- People cannot go where their level of faith cannot take them. In such cases, release God's people with honor so that they leave the battle with their dignity and respect. Realize that some will be just by-standers looking at the fresh move of God from a distance. The Bible says those men who left the battle because of their fear, left in honor but stood at a distance and saw the marvels of God as Gideon was winning the battle then later joined the fight! God can start with the mighty, powerful few who are full of faith and obedience to Him.

<u>Judges 7:2-3</u> "And the LORD said unto Gideon, The people that are with thee are too many for me to give the Midianites into their hands, lest Israel vaunt themselves against me, saying, Mine own hand hath saved me. Now therefore go to, proclaim in the ears of the people, saying, Whosoever is fearful and afraid, let him return and depart early from mount Gilead. And there returned of the people twenty and two thousand; and there remained ten thousand."

A final test was ordered which reduced the army down to a mere 300 men. God finally said that with 300 men He would save His people from the Midianites (Judges 7: 4-7). No doubt some of the men who were dismissed made negative comments about Gideon and questioned his militaristic strategy. The Lord knew His servant was discouraged at this point and told him to take his servant and go to the camp of the Midianites and to listen to what they were saying. God told Gideon that he would be strengthened when he followed those instructions (Judges 7:11).

While listening at the camp site at night, they heard men telling about a strange dream of a cake of barley bread that tumbled into the great camp of Midian and pounded it until it fell and overturned and lay overturned for a long time. The belief was that this was a vision foretelling Midian's defeat – the sword of Gideon, the son of Joash as one with the hand of God (Judges 7:14). The Midianite soldiers were frightened by the news about Gideon overthrowing the altars of Baal and reducing the ranks of his warriors to a shockingly small amount to battle against their huge numbers. These things were unorthodox and paralyzed many of the men in the camp with fear. After seeing this Gideon was reassured that God was moving very strongly on his behalf. Lesson to learn – God will not leave his people comfortless while trusting Him. When his people are in need of strength and encouragement, He will find a way to reassure you that The Lord who is for you is surely victorious over the enemy even before you begin the battle.

Dr. Cecilia Jackson

Gideon left the camp encouraged and returned to his small army to prepare them for the charge. He simply divided them into 3 companies and armed them with trumpets, pitchers that contained burning swords, and when they reached the Midianite camp at midnight they were to blow the trumpets, break the pitchers and at the same time shout the words, "The sword of The Lord, and of Gideon"!!

The men at the camp of Midian were already in a state of trepidation and fretfulness because of the rumors they had heard. So, when suddenly three hundred trumpets blast out into the night, pitchers crash and flaming torches shine into the darkness of the night accompanied by fierce shouts of the Israelites proclaiming, "The Sword of the Lord and of Gideon", it was impossible for the Midianites to discern the strength of their enemy. They believed they were surrounded by an overwhelming force and many began to flee in desperate anguish. Those who tried to hold their ground mistook their fleeing comrades for the men of Israel and fought them fiercely. Israel did not need to fight their enemy; they were slaying each other. By morning, the entire army was in rapid flight to the Jordan River.

Lesson to learn – While there are many, note that the Lord used 300 men to plunder an army of 150,000. He used a simple strategy to win the victory in a battle that would have bloody and vicious; His warriors were not harmed in any way. Today's spiritual battles and strategies are the same. It does not take huge numbers to go forward in God, just the obedient and those who are full of faith. The trumpet of the Lord (the prophetic voice of God speaking to His people and the sound of praise), broken pitchers (vessels, believers who are willing to be broken of their ways and re- made by the hand of The Lord), the flaming sword of the Word of God piercing all darkness, and shouts of victory for you in His name are still preferred strategies of the Lord.

Thirsty believers in our era seam to think it's necessary to seek for new ways to achieve the purpose of God. The Lord has laid in scripture so many examples of what he uses to bring about change, to show Himself strong. We need not waste precious time trying to create what stimulates the intellect and satisfies the yearnings for something strange and new. Look at what The Lord already said and what He has already done, rest from unnecessary labor, Look Back to the Word in order to go forward in God.

Chapter 10
Conclusion

There have been many moves, transitions, periods of change, and obvious shifts of characteristics of the church as she has developed from one era to the next. Questions being asked in today's church are: How do we prepare for another great explosion of the Spirit of God upon the earth through the church? Will God use His church for the next major spiritual explosion in the earth? The Bible says the harvest is ripe, which means people are in the gateway of expectation for intensification of God's power in the earth; but the laborers are few, which means there is a need for Christians/believers to be prepared to do what is necessary to see a supernatural emergence and augmentation of God's power as was seen in the days of old. So, how do believers and how does the church position itself and ready itself for the upcoming yet present harvest? How does the body of Christ prepare for the enlargement and invasion of God's awesome power upon the earth in this generation to meet the demands of the harvest? What is God's expectation of us? What is God's earnest heart about the matter?

The best answer is to look at history and look at the Word of God, the Bible, and see documented patterns of the anointing of God as He transitioned His people in and through major moves in the earth. Look Back to Go forward! These Biblical patterns in history are patterns that highlight principles and principles establish doctrine and set a precedent for expected and anticipated models and standards. What is God's expectation of us? How does the body of Christ prepare for a major move of God in the earth? Look back and study patterns, principles, models and standards; apply those strategies and listen to the voice of the Lord in prayer as He enlightens and breathes on the patterns in His Word in order to walk in the present plan. Study the Biblical prototypes and Step Back, Look Back then Sprint Forward in Kingdom business for The King!

Bibliography

Dialogue Between The Watchmen and The King, Cecilia Jackson
Eternal Church, Bill Hamon
Kingdom Quest, Cecilia Jackson
Position Yourself for Sprinting, Mike Rosenbaum
Present Day Truths, Dick Iverson
The Symbols and Types, Kevin Conner
Wanna Get Fast Track Training, Dan Fichter
Who Am I & Why Am I Here?, Bill Hamon

www.ingramcontent.com/pod-product-compliance
Lightning Source LLC
Chambersburg PA
CBHW071802040426
42446CB00012B/2669